Cover design: Raymond McCullough

Cover photo: Ancient Celtic Shield –

ID 320288385 © Yulia Ryabokon | Dreamstime.com

Faith:

Missing In Action

Dr. Heather Owen

Theotherapist (TT.D, B,Sc., MSc., RGN (Ret'd))

(book #2 in the *Joy Series*)

Published by

Precious Oil

PUBLICATIONS

www.preciousoil.com/publications

ISBN 13: 978-1-7384365-5-2

ISBN 10: 1-7384365-5-1

First published **2026**

Precious Oil

PUBLICATIONS

www.preciousoil.com/publications

10a Listooder Road, Crossgar,

Downpatrick, Northern Ireland BT30 9JE

Contents

Prologue

This brief book looks at the theological and psychological implications of exercising the concept of faith. Exploring our understanding of faith and the difficulties we experience in our execution of it from a Christian worldview. Deepening our understanding of this concept from different perspectives more simply.

It may expose why we struggle with our faith and how to deal with those struggles in a way that will cause us to mature in our relationship to God. It is a journey that is challenging, exciting, frustrating and sometimes confusing, as it is worked out in every walk of life. You are not alone. Every believer goes through times of questioning and believing, all the time, it's not just you! However, this is an opportunity to encourage each other as we entertain these struggles.

Faith in God is an ongoing process until He returns, but it is certain that Christ will not lose the Gift of believers that have been given to Him by our Heavenly Father. **John 17:6**

Introduction

Definition of faith is compared by using different translations to give a fuller understanding.

The well-known verse in **Hebrews 11:1, Youngs Literal Translation, YLT** states *'faith is of things hoped for a confidence, of matters not seen a conviction'*.

'Now faith is the substance of things hoped for, the evidence of things not seen.' **(Hebrews11:1, New King James Version, NKJV)**.

'Now faith is the assurance (the confirmation, the title deed) of the things (we) hoped for (divinely guaranteed), and the evidence of things not seen [the conviction of their reality – faith comprehends as fact what cannot be experienced by the physical senses] ...' **(Hebrews11:1, Amplified Version, AMP)**.

Therefore, faith is the platform and foundation with which everyone has to engage with – everyone has faith in something, which will be explored later.

But these verses from the Bible need to be explained so that they can be applied to daily life. What is the faith that is written about here? The *'confidence'* **(YLT)** describes the ontological basis that the outcome will be favourable, certain, effective and that God is true to His Word; so, reflecting the essence and nature of faith.

The essence of our faith is the outcome of the *'substance'* described in the **NKJV** version. The substance being the qualities needed for the faith to be manifested, the *'things hoped for, the evidence of things not being seen'*.

The Amplified Version suggests it is *'assurance'* that is based in a confirmation of a hopeful expectation. The *'hoped for things'* results in a confidence, confirming as a legal document and is proof. But the proof comes out of the substance of *'hope not seen'*, that is not dependent on material or sensory input.

Therefore, this faith looks to a different reality which brings a conviction not based on senses from this temporary world. A conviction meaning being persuaded by, or a strong belief in the hope that faith brings. So, faith born out of a hopeful expectation increases faith to grow, reinforcing the reality that God's truth brings.

It is an objective reality that is outside of time and space, that is not influenced by sensorial input. Faith therefore has to be centred on and focused on an eternal God because God's essence is outside of time and space. **Genesis 1:1, Isaiah 57:15 Psalm 90:4, Hebrews 11:3** It is a spiritual reality because God is spirit, (**John 4:24**) and thus an absolute reality, which cannot be compared to anything (**Isaiah 40:25-29**) – an absolute reality without any limitations, complete in Himself. So faith in God is certain and sure because God is dependable and immovable, who doesn't change His mind. **Malachi 3:6**

This reality of faith is not influenced by anything worldly, *'by His free grace, it is a gift from God.'* **Philippians 2:10-12**) God, who is based in absolute reality and His gifts are the irrevocable acts which are the *'gifts and the calling of God.'* **Romans 11:29, YLT**

Consequently, we can be certain that God's gift of faith given first enables believers to believe in Him. This gift which is unconditional assures us that we are saved! Now we are partakers of salvation because of the faith given to us. This gift frees us from legalism and all striving.

It's a gift that keeps us in humility, as it is not attained by works, it is not earned, but received and its manifestation is worked out in our lives. The manifestation being the works reflected as a consequence of exercising a faith in God; as God recreates His life in us, by a process of sanctification, **(Philippians**

2:12-13, Hebrews 10:14, YLT) revealing His prepared plan before time. **Psalm 139, AMP**

So, our growing in faith will be a daily experience. Therefore, faith is a daily perseverance that sustains us even if we do not see *'the things asked for'*. It is the *'hope'* of faith, a joyful expectation that keeps us, until we eventually see, with our senses, the things *'asked for'*. Once seen then faith is no longer required.

Sometimes we hold on in faith and do not see its fruition, as we see in **Hebrews 11:39-40**: *'and all these, having obtained a good testimony through faith, did not receive the promise'* which they had stood in faith for. Therefore, we may not see our prayers answered when we think they should be, yet, it is still perceived as faith by God.

This means that faith is based on the action not the outcome – the outcome belonging to God. If this is the case, then we are told that *'God has something better for us'*, a better promise, a heavenly home with our heavenly Father. A perfect promise, *'that they should not be made perfect apart from us,'* – being received along with all the other saints, when Christ returns for His believers

However, this is not the end of living by faith because every day, a saving faith is needed as we engage and encounter different obstacles that life throws at us. **James 1:2-4** The testing of our faith produces the fruits of sanctification, so, *'we walk by faith and not by sight,'* not on the platform of sensory perception. **2 Corinthians 5:7**

Faith is always being stretched, *'from faith to faith'* – so that we can continue to discover the mystery of the greatness of God. **Romans 1:17 ESV** Living by faith challenges our limited world view, helping us to deepen our understanding in accepting the great God that we believe in. And the obstacles we face can take us to the 11th hour before we see the *'things not seen evidenced.'* **Exodus 16:3-4** These *'things'* either being material or spiritual manifestations. The waiting causes us to mature in our faith as it is tested, which deepens our relationship with God.

Struggles of faith are therefore for our benefit, to strip away any self-reliance and self-sufficiency, which we unconsciously depend on, instead of a total dependence on God and God alone. **Luke 17:5-6** *'Some trust in chariots* (military strength) *and some in horses* (power). *But we will remember the name of the Lord our God.'* **Psalm 20:7** *'The horse is prepared for the day of battle, but deliverance is of the Lord.'* **Proverbs 21:31** So, our dependence on God alone is not trusting in any other idol that we think will save us without God.

Subsequently, this faith in the unseen is revealed to us through God the Holy Spirit – the *'Spirit of truth will come and guide us into all truth.'* **John 16:13** The Spirit of God enables us to understand and appreciate all God's gifts given to each one of us to express Christ in us. **1 Corinthians 2:9-13**

And it is the Holy Spirit that regenerates our hearts and renews us, *'not by works that are in righteousness that we did, but according to His kindness, He did save us, through a bathing of regeneration, and a renewing of the Holy Spirit.'* **Titus 3:5 YLT** But by a therapeutic process that takes place internally in our spirits causing us to be changed from glory to glory: *'our outward man is perishing, yet the inward man is being renewed day by day.'* **2 Corinthians 3:18, 4:16**

This encourages us as our internal spiritual reality becomes real to us as we engage with it and are transformed by it. This therapeutic transformation takes place when we deny ourselves and surrender to God working within us. *'If we put our faith in him then we must deny ourselves and take up His cross.'* **Luke 14:26 AMP**

However, each believer is given a measure of faith in the gifts given to them, but how is faith measured? Is the measure of faith, the judgement we place on the outcome of the gift exercised, working itself out in each believer? If so, who does the judging and by which measure? Let's explore this together.

–

1 – Losing your first love

First saved –

'I know your works, your labour, and patience and that you cannot bear those who are evil. And you have tested those who say they are apostles and are not, and have found them liars; and you have persevered and have patience, and have laboured for My name's sake and have not become weary.' **Revelation 2:2-3**

'Nevertheless, I have this against you, that you have left your first love. Remember therefore from where you have fallen; repent and do the first works, or else I will come to you quickly and remove your lamp-stand from its place – unless you repent. But this you have, that you hate the deed of the Nicolaitans, which I also hate.' **Revelation 2:4-6**

Acts 19 first introduces us to the Ephesians when Paul was on his missionary journey. Paul encouraged them to move on in their understanding of God and the baptism of the Holy Spirit. The Ephesians had only known John's baptism, so they were baptised in the name of the Lord Jesus, and Paul laid hands on them, so that *'the Holy Spirit came upon them, and they spoke with tongues and prophesied.'* **Acts 19:1-7**

Through the Apostle Paul the Ephesians had been warned *'that savage wolves will come in among you, not sparing the flock. Also, from among yourselves men will rise up, speaking perverse things, to draw away the disciples after themselves.'* **Acts 20:28-31** So, it is not a surprise that they worked hard and laboured to keep the truth, by drawing a line between those who claim that they are apostles and are liars.

This group toiled against the gospel from being distorted and endured, despite the controversy that they found themselves up against. And it states that they did not become weary in standing for truth, even though from the first time that Paul met them to the writing of Revelation a long time had passed but they didn't give up standing up for the truth!

Yet, in their service for God and standing for the truth, something happened to them without realising it. **They lost their first love.** How is it possible that in the fight, these new disciples in standing for truth, managed to lose the very truth that gave them the freedom and joy, to serve God and to discern those who were lying and actively working *'against God's truth?'*

Is it possible that to be so zealous for the gospel and defending the truth, that they forgot the application of the blessing of the gospel towards themselves and their relationship with their Saviour?

The battle belongs to the Lord (**1 Samuel 17:47**) so if this is true that the Lord always wins the battle; why do so many believers in standing for the truth lose their first love? If the battle belongs to the Lord, then the victory is always His and ours. So, our faith is exercised when we remember the victory is ours, even if it is not seen in reality yet.

Can you remember when you were first saved, or came to a realisation that God died for you paid the penalty for your sins and forgave you? When you first believed, and now have been given new life and a new relationship with your Saviour; experiencing the joy and peace at that moment? Knowing that you are now justified before your Saviour, accepted by Him in the power of His love, full of the Holy Spirit and free from the guilt and condemnation of sin from the enemy.

'There is now no condemnation to those that believe.' **Romans 8:1** This summary after the battle and ongoing struggles between the flesh and the spirit within the believer (**Romans 7**) leaves Paul in a state of wretchedness. And the qualification does not need to be added to it, *'who do not walk according to the flesh but according to the Spirit.'* **Romans 8:1b** (not in the *textus receptus*) This addition suggests that our new relationship is dependent on what we may or may not do.

And because of this freedom, you wanted to please God, to serve Him and spread the gospel to others who haven't shared your new faith and life yet. So, we start off enthusiastic, eager to serve, ready to fulfil all the potential that God has created in you. Experiencing a new measure of your worth in Christ, fully confident that you belong to Him and He to you. **John17:9-12** This new relationship that no one can take away and nothing can come in between, *'who shall separate us from the love of Christ.'* **Romans 8:33-39**

So, headlong straight into works of service we enter, fully committed and so full of joy that seemingly nothing can take it away. However, over time the service becomes a chore and the freedoms become a shackle, as we engage with those who don't want to listen, or those who don't want to engage with our new found faith and relationship with God. The honey-moon period is over so the nostalgia and initial excitement of your relationship with God is diminished.

The difficulties come and the storms may overwhelm us, so we retreat and the blessings of the new relationship with Christ become distant to us – but we are believers who know the truth and know the right path to follow, therefore, we cannot stop believing; so, we become less enthusiastic and slowly become half hearted.

We still believe, but that same joy and peace is slowly vanishing as we serve God. We lose our first love and seem oblivious to it, as we engage in more service or works, to keep up the momentum. Are we now in works righteousness? Is this the reason for the loss we feel? Have we traded in a substitute to cover up for the losses we may be experiencing? Or did we have a wrong view of our acceptance in Christ?

Loss is difficult to manage if our theology is not founded in the Word of God. Our losses are connected to our possessions and these reflect our identity, giving us a sense of our security in life. Therefore, if our identity is not found in Christ our security will be tenuous, so we try to possess our possessions to prevent loss. So, when we lose our possessions, we can become destabilised emotionally because it challenges us at the core of who we are, our identity, creating instability, making us feel insecure and vulnerable.

But the truth is we can lose everything, however we can never lose Christ, because it is He who holds onto us. **John17:12** This means that if God has called us we cannot be lost. *'By this we know that we abide in Him, and He is us, because He has given us of His Spirit.'* **1 John 4:13-19**

So, maybe our misunderstanding of God's Word may cause us to lose our first love because we won't have that *'assurance'* that the AMP version speaks of. So, our *'assurance'* must be based in faith in God, to sustain our first love. Therefore, the loss of our first love can be restored when our theological understanding is correct that is not emotionally dependent. To love is to accept another without the need for them having to prove themselves, it is unconditional acceptance as Christ loved us! **1 John 4:19**

To love God is to accept His love, His forgiveness, His new life within, His Holy Spirit's work within us, to accept His truth. Faith that is built on a lie of false hope is guaranteed to lose a first love. A false hope that makes claims about what God will do that is taken out of context from His Word.

For example, the overused verse – that the plans God has for you is to prosper you … was taken out of context, as Jeremiah told them to, *'build houses and dwell in them, plant gardens and eat their fruit, take wives and beget sons and daughters; and take wives for your sons and give your daughters to husbands, so that they may bear sons and daughters that you may be increased there and not diminished and seek the peace of the city where I have caused you to be carried away captive and pray to the Lord for it, for in its peace you will have peace.'*

This was spoken while they were in exile. **Jeremiah 29:5-7** I'm not sure anyone in exile at the time of writing would consider they were prospering, given peace and a future of hope. SEVENTY years in captivity is a long time to hold onto a hope for the future, so it's not surprising that other false prophets came along with feel good sounding words, to encourage the people, but their words were deceptive and lies. **Jeremiah 29:8-9** But these false prophets met their end under Nebuchadnezzar. **Jeremiah 29:21**

This apostasy of *'cherry picking'* the Word of God that makes us feel good about ourselves'. For example, *'For where two or three are gathered together in My name, I am there in the midst of them.'* **Matthew 18:20** Yet, Elijah said to the people, *'I, even I only, am left a prophet of the LORD, but Baal's prophets are 450 men.'* **1 Kings 18:22** So, God can do miracles even if there is only one person of God praying!

Other areas of misinterpretation of the Word, are in asking God for things, in answers to prayer, *'Ask, and it will be given to you; seek, and you will find; knock, and it will be opened to you.'* **Matthew 7:7** But we don't get everything we ask for, because in other places, it is conditional on being in God's will, or we ask with wrong motives.

Or in healing, *'And the prayer of faith will save the sick, and the Lord will raise him up.'* **James 5:14ff** So, does that mean the sick don't have faith to be healed?

There are many examples of *'cherry picking'* in the Bible, to gravitate to verses that give us a feel-good factor that we like but ignore and avoid those we don't.

So, we can learn from this that we must take the **whole counsel of God**. If not, it sets people up for disappointment and failure with an unconscious demand to have to do more, to achieve our own ends, so our striving increases to retrieve that first love – a man-made striving that negates the faith given by God.

This tragedy of loss needs to be reclaimed by not listening to the false prophets with their false hopes and teachings, *'according to their own desires because they have itching ears ... and they will turn their ears away from the truth, and be turned aside to fables.'* **2 Timothy 4:3-4**

2 – Groups that God hates?

Who were the Nicolaitans and why did God hate them? Nicolaitan in Greek means, *'a destructive people'*. The name is derived from the Greek *nikolaos*, meaning *'conqueror of the people'*, or *'to overcome'*, or *'one who subdues the people'* – combining *nikos, nikao* (victory) and *laos* (people).

The Nicolaitans followed a man called Nicolaus, mentioned in **Acts 6:5 YLT**. It was a sect that was condemned because they followed idolatrous behaviours and committed sexual immorality. Their practices were similar to the prophet Balaam (**Numbers 22-25, Revelation 2:14-16**), who could be manipulated to prophesy whatever was asked of him. He was used by King Balak to curse Israel and to put a stumbling block before them. The guise of religious belief without questioning the telling, opens the door to leading people astray and away from God. In the same way Nicolaus fell to deception – his fall was a lesson to us all.

It seems that the Nicolaitans compromised with idolatrous practices, imitating pagan feasts (**Exodus 20:3, 1 Corinthians 10:21**), and engaged in sexual immorality. **1 Corinthians 6:18, 1 Thessalonians 4:3-5** They distorted the gospel of grace into permissive licence to sin (**Jude 4, 2 Peter 2:19**), and engaged in liberties which eroded God's holiness amongst his people. (**Strongs: 3531**) Their conduct was even questioned by the early church fathers: Irenaeus quotes them as *'un-restrained indulgence'* (**Heresies 1.26.3**), along with others – Hippolytus and Clement of Alexandria – reinforcing the moral decline of the Nicolaitans.

It is thought that Nicolaus was one of the seven chosen to serve at the tables, a man full of wisdom and of the Holy

Spirit. Yet, despite these qualities he led himself and others astray.

How could this man who was once full of the Holy Spirit and wisdom, end up propagating a sect that was hated by God? The moral decline and distortion of an expression of love was manipulated, resulting and ending in opposition to the purity of God's love. Yet, he was a man full of the Holy Spirit? How could he fall for this deception and trade in a substitute that could only destroy and bring harm to all those who engaged in it?

Love is precious and **1 Corinthians 13** is a text known by many, with its qualities of love – God's love, Agape love – a love that builds up and enhances the individual so that it can be given to others. This kind of love is the highest form of love and can only be attained as we receive God's love. Love that is forced onto others is not God's love; it is manipulation and coercive misplaced power and control.

God's Agape love allows us to confront the internal conflicts that would draw us away from Him. This love is meant to flow freely from God to us, from us to others to return to God, a love that delights to follow God's commands.

Before we were saved, we engaged in behaviours that were against God, but now we choose to please Him and abide by His rules, to live holy lives – an impossibility if the service and works engaged in come from our own effort; even though this outward expression may appear noble and righteous or impressive to others.

So, *'do I now persuade men, or God? Or do I seek to please men? For if I still persuade men, I would not be a bond-servant of Christ.'* **Galatians 6:10** We were not saved to works alone but because of our new found faith and life in God. This will be reflected in our works of service – this is not wrong, but the issue is the origin of the nature of the works – to please men or God? Good works are good if the origin – the source – is not based in internal pathology (sickness) and therefore is right before God. We can be impressed by the good works because we can wrongly discern they may be from God. Good works don't save us and never will. And a good work that violates God's commands, to be all He has created us to be, with the gifts He has given to us, amounts to disobedience and is not sourced from God's love. **Genesis 3.6ff**

This type of service always leads to compromise and trying to *'fit in'*, resulting in being less than God created us to be! Therefore, when we engage in this kind of service we open the door to *'loneliness'*; it doesn't satisfy because compromise never fulfils the plans and purposes that God has for us. Compromise always weakens our faith as we try to accommodate others to meet our personal perceived goals.

However, bad works seem obvious to all! This is why the Nicolaitans were hated by God, their works were against God and consequentially destroyed individuals who indulged in them. But they, like us when we indulge in substitutes to compensate for God's true love, gradually move away from the ideal of God's Agape and lose our first love. It's subtle, it's gradual – we don't notice it at first, but God does. That relationship we longed for, enjoyed, and the peace and freedom that came with its new life, gradually slips away.

We still believe – but not like we used to. Could this lack of our first love be a process of maturity in Christ, or a process of compromise to fulfil our needs without God's help?

If the former, then the answer could suggest a more mature, stable, secure understanding of the process of God drawing us into a deeper relationship with Him. Is this true? Do you feel more stable, more secure, more at peace and free in your relationship with God?

Or are you of the latter mind that has sought elsewhere for God's love to meet your needs, by engaging in other substitutes for God, e.g. the cultural philosophies of today's zeitgeist to justify the substitutes in the guise of progressivism, or some other form of liberalism? Has this stance drawn you closer to God or further away from Him and a loss of your first love?

What would progressive ideas look like? – accepting cultural values that are opposed in the Bible, *'in the name of love'*? Acceptance of individuals without boundaries – anything goes! Love is love; let's all get along and love each other. Surely, a biblical concept?

God commands us to love one another, to love our neighbours as ourselves. **Mark 12:31 YLT** But the true love of God is conditional on obedience to His Word and keeping His laws. Progressive ideas are a misunderstanding and a distortion of God's love. God's Agape love is pure and holy and therefore must be aligned to His Word.

So, is Nicolaitinism a form of rebellion? – an antinomian spirit that goes against God's truth, to engage in an idolatrous substitute form of religion that ends up compromising faith and of love towards God? How do we deal with this? The Ephesians in **Revelation 2** were commended for their stance in discerning false apostles, false teachings and the heresies of the Nicolaitans – yet they lost their first love!

We still believe that GOD IS LOVE, but our half-heartedness means the application strangely falls away, as we open the door to the lies of the enemy. Our faith is in the God of love, who has saved us from ourselves from all the negative effects of sins destruction and demise. This is good – however, moving towards idolatrous substitutes may set up an impression of maturity in Christ – for example by presenting as knowledgeable, biblical teachers that may cause others to interpret this as maturity; yet, be a confidence that comes from ourselves and is not from God.

'Place no confidence or dependence [in what we have or who we are] in the flesh (and on outward privileges and physical advantages and external appearances.)' **Philippians 3:3 AMP** So, our reliance becomes on what we know about God, but not on our personal relationship with God.

Chapter 2 – Groups that God hates?

God first loved us so we can love Him. **1 John 4:19** But this love must permeate through every part of our being, *'Since by your obedience to the Truth through the [Holy] Spirit you have purified your hearts for the sincere affection of the brethren, [see that you] love one another fervently from a pure heart'* (**1 Peter 1:22 AMP**) – without hypocrisy, with a sincere love earnestly.

Yet, we struggle to love each other, or ourselves, and God. The result of this is that we are mindful that we all still have a sinful nature that is battling against the Holy Spirit's guidance, that challenges our souls to be in line with God's Spirit in His Word. **Romans 7 AMP** And this sinful nature must be addressed, despite the fact that we are already saved, but like Cain, *'sin crouches at your door; its desire is for you, but you must master it.'* **Genesis 4:7 AMP**

Because the presence of sin will corrupt and turn us away from the first love we received when we first believed. So, the process of *'we have been saved, are being saved and will be saved'* continues until Christ returns.

In some religious circles, e.g. the holiness movement, there is a denial that new believers can now be sinners. This means that the consequences of sin are not dealt with, and the ensuing loss of the first love increases and becomes evident, as *'works righteousness'* overtake us.

There are also the over-exaggerations and immature responses that any expression of sin is demonic and must be exorcised. These extremes do not retrieve the first love that is lost; they are both heresies which leave believers in a state of delusion, or are made to feel guilty and condemned.

The latter heresy opens the door to the believer that they are vulnerable to the negative spiritual world, which can hinder their walk with God – as if the devil is stronger or greater than God! **1 John 4:4**

Exorcism of a suspected demonic sin allows some excitable leaders a position of control and dominance over believers, which is a form of spiritual abuse.

As believers, we must acknowledge that we have sinned and continue to fall short. **Romans 3:23-24** The former erroneous belief has crept in that thinks that now we are saved we are OK – an error that leads to a self-righteous belief that our good works will give credence to our faith in Christ.

It also springs up out of the latter that a deliverance from the demonic will free us to return to our first love. Except, if it IS demonic and IS exorcised, but the emotional foundation is not dealt with, then that first love cannot return until the emotional and psychological platform is healed. **Luke 11:24ff, Matthew 12:43ff** We are saved, righteous and holy in God's eyes – however, we are not like Christ yet, so there is more work for God to do.

To love without hypocrisy, is to recognise that we are all sinners, yet God loves us and saves us, for Himself and His purposes. **Ephesians 2:10** God saved us while we were sinners and loves us as we were. **Romans 5:8** God is under no illusion about who we are, or how He can refine us to be more like Christ! He knows what we need and when to meet those needs according to His purposes and timing.

Is the loss of our first love for God, a divine intervention? – in that, this new creature with its new-found faith and love in God, now has to be confronted with the things within us that will disturb and inhibit a deeper walk in the knowledge and love of who God is? *'But whatever comes out of the mouth comes from the heart, and this is what makes a man unclean and defiles him. For out of the heart come evil thoughts [reasoning and disputing's and designs] such as murder, adultery, sexual vice, theft, false witnessing, slander and irreverent speech.'* **Matthew 15:18-20 AMP**

Therefore, does the loss of our first love expose an idea of love that is fallacious? This idea exposes a symbolic form of love that Eric Fromm refers to in his book, *'The Art of Loving'* (**1956**). So losing this symbolic ideation of love is helpful because it undermines God's Agape love.?

We saw in the Nicolaitans an obvious distortion of that love, but is God exposing that distortion of love in us too? We may not possibly have gone to the behavioural extremes of the Nicolaitans, but may still struggle internally with the understanding of what true love is? And this internal struggle is what God uses to draw us into a fuller understanding of His Agape Love.

3 – Faith in what?

Faith is a gift given by God. We all have faith and that faith is interpreted and projected onto different things. For example, some have faith in material things e.g. in chairs we sit on, or in material possessions. Some have faith in supernatural things, e.g. aliens, UFOs, etc. Some have faith in their ideologies, some have faith in themselves, some have faith in science, some have faith in God. So which faith is the faith we are talking about here?

Faith that we are speaking about in this book is the faith that is given by His Holy Spirit to believe in God. **1 Corinthians 12:4-11, 2 Corinthians 4:13** This faith is a gift given by God that is necessary to please Him *'and without faith, it is impossible to please Him, for whoever would draw near to God must believe that He exists, and that He rewards those who seek Him.'* **Hebrews 11:6 ESV** This faith, which sustains us every day, is a faith in God. **Habbakuk 2:4, Mark 11:22**

But who is God? Our understanding of our belief in God may challenge our belief systems, as to what or why we believe what we do. A belief system is *'a mental acceptance of and conviction in the truth, actuality, or validity of something. Anything that is believed or accepted as true'.* (**The American Heritage Dictionary, 2012**)

So, our belief systems can be highly subjective and emotionally based – or objective, logical and rational. These two realities may clash with each other in our minds, as in Psycho-clashing. (**Rivera, Christian Counselling International**)

This can be a complex discussion as our belief systems have been influenced by many factors. These different influences can confuse, contradict, undermine or reinforce our belief systems; therefore, it is vital that these are in line with what the Bible teaches, so that we can remain stable and secure in our personalities. The question to be asked is, are we holding onto right or wrong beliefs and who is the arbitrator of these?

So, God's word comes up against our belief systems, which can challenge and may distress us, if our beliefs are not in line with God's truth. When exposed the discomfort produces a cognitive dissonance that may cause us to reject the belief we held. This may cause us to take on a paradigm shift – changing our belief systems – or it can reinforce the biblical view that we believe in, that is based on the Word which we have relied on and stood on for a long time.

Many influences from different sources can create confusion and possible crisis of the faith we uphold.

First formed beliefs come from our significant figures – our parents. Subconsciously, we take on board interjects as children, without even realising or understanding it. Then as we grow up, we engage with the wider society and other cultural belief systems. Then we engage with our peers who influence us with group think and the pressure of group dynamics.

Or we engage with educational systems with different philosophies, ideas and theories which give other perspectives. All of the above contributing to a conglomerate mixed bag of belief systems that we try to navigate and interpret, as we incorporate and engage with them in our daily walk of faithful experiences.

Parental influences are significant in the sense that they affect us at the core of our being. Our personalities are moulded and manipulated from the day we are born. These influences become deeply ingrained in our core being.

Subconsciously, we may not be aware of the way we have been affected by them; as we have assimilated them and diagnosed ourselves as a type of personality. E.g. Jung's introverted or extroverted personality type, **(Berry, 2000)**, which we may hide behind to justify our response with others. This self-diagnosis allows us to hide behind our *'weaknesses'* and *'flaws'* – labelling and ruling ourselves in or out to engage in particular activities, e.g. *'I can't stand up at the front and sing in the worship group because I'm an 'introvert''* (or a … whatever the blank fill in is).

These personality traits also filter through to group activities that take on a different force and momentum, which are projected and may continue into the future, e.g. groups may hold long term feuds, prejudices or grudges against others long expressed in the past. This can be obvious to the outsider but these groups can give their self-confessed reasons why their ideas are held today.

When confronted by the lack of reasoning behind the grudges, prejudices etc., it can create deep animosity by exposing the futility and ignorance of held views that is not applicable to the present relationship, e.g. family groups that don't relate to other members in the family because of something that happened years ago, even though the exposure of their reasoning is irrational.

So, any group can be subject to this irrationality where it exposes position and status within that group setting. Alfred Adler discusses many personality types and how they interact in birth order, e.g. first-borns – the eldest may take on a leadership role, so they take up that position in the group and can be very overbearing and manipulative. Or the last born, who takes on a dependency role in the group, manipulating the group to feel sorry for them, and playing the victim.

Or the middle born that missed the attention from their significant figures, so can become the drama queens, exhibiting histrionics, etc. Obviously above are simplified generalisations but the point is that birth position can determine how an individual fits into a group setting. Groups adopt different styles which express some personality types better for the individuals involved in that particular group setting.

When a new belief system is accepted, it can create a paradigm shift that turns the individual's world upside down, e.g. as in a religious conversion experience, i.e. from atheism, or Islam, to Christianity, or a different denomination, etc. This shift may cause dramatic consequences and rejection from the societal group that was once accepting of the individual.

To go against the cultural norms of the society in which you live, can lead to being ostracised and persecuted. The suffering this produces can be intense and may drive the individual to find another culture in which to live, for fear of imprisonment or being attacked or even murdered. Cultural influences have a force of their own, the mob rule and if you *'go against the tide'* you may feel the full force of this position.

Standing up for belief systems that are held onto can invite a *'them and us'* scenario, exacerbating the situation. This sets up an embattlement and combative approach that can escalate into local or national disturbances, within and without the church setting.

'Groups have power, but a large number in the group, or their ability to influence others will evoke a reaction when they express their beliefs. These will either be measures for or against them.' (from **Wikipedia**: *group think)* But who decides if the *'group think'* is reasonable or rational. This is a problem in a relativistic cultural society, each group believing that their belief system or ideology is right and the others are all wrong. Polarisation of these extremes of expression increases the combative tone and anger to prove that the relativist view or held belief is right.

The ability to discuss issues helps to keep a society with different ideas more cohesive. Without middle ground and a rational basis for discussion – which happens with identity politics – society will be more divided and separated, with unfashionable identities marginalised. Therefore, what we believe and why may clash with other ideologies, so we need a space in which to discuss these, so that the separation and divisions are dispelled.

Chapter 3 – Faith in what?

Leadership has a considerable influence on our expectations and if the leader has been a poor example, then this will affect individuals' perceptions of whether to trust their leaders. Leaders are put in place by God (**Romans13:1-2 YLT**) to represent God to the people they serve – however, they can be corrupted by their own issues and misuse their power and authority (more later). **1 Samuel 13:14**

Our earliest influence of leadership begins in the home – fathers and mothers are set up to represent God to their children. If the father's representation is an abuse of the power God has entrusted to them then this can disturb the child's relationship to their Heavenly Father. A child who has a father who is distant and emotionally unavailable will project that example onto God, therefore their relationship with God will be distant. A child who has a controlling father will project that example onto God causing the child to be afraid of God in the wrong way, creating an insecure relationship.

A child who has an absent father – who is in the home, but not there – will also have difficulties in their relationship with God, questioning is God someone who cares for them or who can be depended on? Conversely, this applies to a mother's example too. Therefore, parents need to address their own issues so that they can minimise the conflicts that they project onto their children. However, these are generalisations but seen in many instances of the parent/child relationship and their projection onto God.

Consequently, the projection of our beliefs onto God due to bad examples of leadership can distort the basis and foundation of our faith. If we have judged by what we have experienced and seen in leadership, our faith can and may be influenced, distorted and dependent on what we have witnessed. The deficit from a true and right representation by those who represent God can set up a conditional expectation for salvation.

If God is not seen or heard in the home, or love is not manifested as God shows us, then the challenge is on God to perform to meet that deficit. For example, if the representation is not seen, then the believer distorts and expects God to be seen, to answer prayers, to do miracles, heal people, etc. If so, then the foundation of faith can be shaken and unstable because, as already discussed previously, *'faith is the substance of things not seen'*.

An unstable and unreliable faith is what James speaks of in **James 1:6-8**. A double minded believer is unstable in all his ways and doubts, uncertain about everything he thinks, feels, decides about his own faith. He is like a wave of the sea being driven by wind and tossed around.

An unstable faith trusting in what is seen, is contrary to **Hebrews 11:1** – having a faith that is *'hoped for'* and evidenced by ***'what is not seen'***. If your faith is dependent on what is seen, it is not totally dependent on God and not real. If it is conditionally dependent on answers, then it is emotionally based and culturally influenced by materialism and secularism. Jesus said, *'Thomas because you have seen me, you have believed; Blessed are those who have not seen, and yet have believed.'* **John 20:24-29**

Leadership examples are not just seen in the home but in many forms of authority, e.g. education, employment, health-care, financial institutions, governance with politicians local and national, church denominations, cultural influences, etc, and if the leadership concept has already been tainted, this can be projected onto authority figures within these settings.

However, the faith that is dependent on God is a faith dependent on the absolute truth, which is an objective faith, the essence of reality. If we reject the truth of God's word and keep our misaligned truth, the result will be to compromise or change the truth of God.

This is a slippery path to engage on, as rejection of some of God's truth will make it easier and lead to rejecting more of God's Word. If we move towards compromising, we err towards a liberal view of Christianity where anything goes. In the name of including all beliefs systems we are left with little truth at all. Our faith in God becomes the weaker for it. Only standing on God's truth in His Word provides a solid and secure foundation for us, to bring stability and security.

Conversely, adhering to the Word of God without any grace, leads to a legalistic type of faith which can become very controlling, authoritative and harsh. Therefore, God's Word must be applied as absolute truth but with grace and love.

Belief in God's word is therefore exclusive because there is ONLY ONE TRUTH!

4 – Going deeper with God

Therefore, what and whom we believe is important to enable our faith to grow and mature.

But again, who is this God that gives us this faith? Our understanding of *'God'* will influence how we deal with the complexities of life. So, if our understanding does not match the written Word as revealed in the Bible, then the foundation of our faith will be fragile and weak. We will not be able to stand strong if there is a cognitive dissonance, as we will continue to fight against our doubts, unbelief and rejection of God.

We have been created and saved FOR HIS PURPOSES AND PLANS (**Proverbs 16:4, Ephesians 1:11**) – not ours, and we will say we agree with this until it clashes with our understanding of how God should work in our lives. This psycho-clashing (**Rivera**) brings out the confusion and negativity of our sinful natures which is in enmity against God. Therefore, when this clash is revealed we need to face it, address it therapeutically as to its origin, so that God can heal us from deep within and transform our lives – going deeper with God. **Psalms 42:5-7, Hebrews 12:15**

The example we are given is from our Saviour, '*not my will but your will be done.'* **Luke 22:42** Jesus surrendered to the purposes and plans of His Father in Heaven. We are even given the example of the Lord's prayer, *'your Kingdom come, your will be done, in Heaven as on Earth.'* **Matthew 6:10**

The reign of God in our lives is going to bring us into conflict with Him at some time or another, therefore, we need to be prepared to deal with this in a therapeutic way that causes us to enter into that deeper relationship with God.

The consequence of not addressing these clashes will take us down a path of rejecting God or pushing Him into lip-service only, but this doesn't have to happen. **Isaiah 29:13, Matthew 15:8-12**

Our knowledge of God's purposes and plans may conflict with our perspective of what we believe about God working in our lives. But why do we think that we have greater knowledge than God? **Job 38-40:1-2** In humility, we have to accept that our knowledge and our understanding is limited (**Psalms139:6, Romans11:33, 1 Corinthians 13:12**) and cannot even begin to compare our knowledge with God.

Isaiah 40 quotes *'to whom do you compare me.'* **Isaiah 40:12-18** There is no comparison, not even with our own intellect, knowledge and understanding. To believe that we know what is best and good for us, is pride. To struggle against God is to lose! And to fight God is to experience mental distress and emotional instability. Believers who are in this position will be humbled by the mighty hand of God.

Our Saviour will set us up on a path to enable us to come face to face with ourselves, so that we surrender to Him. **2 Samuel 24:14 YLT** Surrendering to and accepting God's purposes and plans when they don't agree with ours is a sign of humility, maturity, and healing.

Our Heavenly Father who loves us and is continually saving us until He returns will discipline us, if needed, so that we become more like Him. **Hebrews 12:3-11** This disciplining can be a painful process but is confirmation that our Father God cares enough about us and loves us enough to take us through this process.

If we try and fight against God and resist Him; this will be a futile endeavour, because God is greater and His purposes will be worked out in our lives. In the end, God who sent His son to die for us will have His way, He is always in control because He is Sovereign. However, despite many believers claiming to believe that God is Sovereign, when *'the rubber hits the road'* and the trials come, it is disputed.

So, do we truly believe in God's Sovereignty and if so, why do we become distressed when life doesn't go our way in our understanding of how things should be worked out in our lives. This psycho-clashing challenges us as we work it out every day. Therefore, having a biblical understanding of hermeneutics (the interpretation of scripture) will enable us to uphold God's Sovereignty and trust His rule and reign over us.

However, our sinful nature may resist God's will in our lives, leading us to internal distress, causing us to move away from God and separate ourselves from Him. This results in erring towards our own resources, becoming self-reliant, self-serving and increasingly independent from God. Paul is a great example of this as he exclaims in **Romans7:24**, *'O wretched man that I am! Who will deliver me from this body of death?'* When we believe in a Saving God, He not only becomes our Saviour but He becomes our Sovereign God, Lord and Master over our lives.

God's ways are far better and higher than our ways, *'For my thoughts are not your thoughts, neither are your ways my ways. As the heavens are higher than the earth, so are my ways higher than your ways and my thoughts than your thoughts.'* **Isaiah 55:8-9** God's thoughts towards us are of peace, not of evil, to give us a future and a hope, but maybe not in the way we expect! **Jeremiah 29:11-14**

Once we recognise and acknowledge our sin this can be dealt with. We need to ask for God's forgiveness, thinking that we know better than God. To repent of our pride and any thoughts of self-reliance, self-securities, self – *'anything'*; thinking that we can handle life without God; a recipe for disaster!

God in us works through us, so we can conquer all things, but it's Him doing the work – we are the vessels of clay that God chooses to work through, so that the excellence of the power may be of God and not of us. **Isaiah 45:9, 2 Corinthians 4:7ff** We are imperfect vessels that have been contaminated by our sinful natures, yet God chooses to work out His plans through us. Therefore, we do not lose heart, because outwardly man is perishing, yet inwardly man is being renewed day by day. **Romans7:18 2 Corinthians 4:16** Truly a miracle indeed!

Subsequently, His plans will lead us into circumstances that may expose our *'sinful nature.'* The trials we face test our faith, so we can count it all joy as it profits us – producing patience, perfection, completeness, lacking nothing, perfecting our faith, so we can rejoice that God is exposing our sin to perfect us and transform us. **James 1:2ff, Romans 12:1-2 AMP** The tribulations reveal what is lacking within us; so that God can produce the Christ-centred attributes that reveal many things – including things like perseverance, character, hope. **Romans 5:3-5**

Have your circumstances or relationships brought up hidden agendas, doubts, unbelief, injustices, anger, etc., against God? Whatever is revealed is God's purpose and part of His perfect plan to expose our wrong believing, theology and sinful nature within. This is why the Word states in **Romans 5:2-5**, *'we rejoice in the hope of the glory of God and this hope does not disappoint us'* – because of God's love being poured into our hearts by the Holy Spirit, who was given to us!

God isn't interested in external behavioural modification; He desires the transforming power of the renewing of our minds – that is the whole of our personalities – the inner heart towards Him. This is how we know God's will; it is an internal change which is reflected externally.

Our understanding of *'love'* is challenged as God takes us through His purposes and plans. Does God really *'love'* us if He plans for us to suffer for His purposes? Yet, suffering is a part of His plan, as Christ suffered and died. 'He learned obedience through His suffering,' (**Hebrews 5:8**) – so will we!

'For He who the Lord loves He chastens and scourges every son who he received, if you endure chastening God is dealing with you as children of God ... Shall we not much

more readily be in subjection to the Father of spirits and live? ... and our chastening is for our profit ... so we may take part in His holiness..... no chastening is joyful in the present but painful..... but reveals the peaceful fruit of God's righteousness, to those who have been trained by it!' **Hebrews 12:6-11**

Have we been badly taught by leaders? *'Come to Jesus and everything will be fine'* theology? *'God works all things out for good'* (**Romans 8:29**) theology? – missing out *'according to His purposes'!* Or that, we are *'being conformed to the image of His Son'* – an ongoing process. **v.29** Or shall tribulation separate us from God, (**v.35**) and *'for your sake we are killed all day long; we are accounted as sheep for the slaughter!'* Sadly, the truth of these verses can be ignored to accommodate and compromise people to come to *'faith'*, but this faith is no faith at all, as it is built on a very shaky foundation.

Is working out our faith a challenge? Yes, but we are told to work it out with *'fear and trembling,'* **Philippians 2:12-13** remembering that *'it is God who works in you both to will and to do for His good pleasure'*. God is the giver of faith, so that His purposes and plans will be worked out. Therefore, we do not have to strive, but our part is to deal with the psycho-clashing which manifests from within. Striving to put ourselves right will be a man-made effort – so we surrender to God who enables us to be transformed to be right with Him.

Are the doubts a projection onto God from significant figures, or previous representative leaders in the church? If so, identify the root of the relationship and use the therapeutic tools to heal. Is the unbelief, a trust issue? If so, identify the relationship conflict which birthed this distrust. Is it a distortion of love? If so, identify the relational conflict, to deal with the distortive root. The Bible states that *'the root of all bitterness leads to defilement'* as stated.

Did God let you down, disappoint you, betray you? Then what were your expectations of God? Are they grounded in bad theology? Have you been taken captive to a vain philosophical view of holiness? For example, do you serve God, expecting a reward in Heaven; this is based in a cognitive fallacy that if you serve God you will be rewarded in a particular way? The workers at the vineyard also had this problem, citing injustices and unfairness, in receiving the same wage as the late comers. **Matthew 20:1-16 AMP**

Was your obedience a conditional obedience, (**Matthew 21:28-32 AMP**) a self-proclaimed righteousness out of service to the father, an expectation of being treated differently to the younger son? Serving God out of a sense of duty? Is this a legalistic approach to serving God? Is it possible that your belief in God projected unrealistic and unbiblical expectations onto God?

At the end of **Hebrews 11** we read how disciples held onto faith even though they didn't receive the promises made to them – others refused to recant their faith in God, even though it meant death. Can we learn from them that faith is not about a reward here on earth, a cognitive distortion, but our reward is in God in Heaven, that we are waiting for?

God challenges our temporal, quick fix gratifications, instant desires and rewards to a purpose that far excels these momentary pleasures. We are more than this earth, we belong to a heavenly King. We are His subjects, who bow to His Sovereignty even if it hurts our flesh.

We are of a different world, our spirits are seated with Him in Heavenly places. **Ephesians 2:4-7 AMP**

5 – God's silence!

God exposes the differences between this temporal world and His eternal world, by adopting different strategies with different individuals, to enable them to address and contend with this chasm.

One strategy is in the use of prayer. We are told *'ask and it shall be given to you, seek and you will find, knock and the door will be opened to you.'* **Matthew7:7** Yet, the reality is that God's timing and ours are vastly different. We have high expectations from this verse that God will answer, but in our minds it is always now, or in the very near future – however, when these prayers are not answered in the way we think, we start to lose our faith and doubts creep in.

Matthew 27:46 – even at the cross, God the Father seemed silent, as Jesus cries out, 'MY GOD, MY GOD WHY HAVE YOU FORSAKEN ME'? He implores God, *'Why are you so far from helping me and from the words of my groaning? O my God, I call out by day but you do not answer; and by night, but I find not rest nor quiet.'* **Psalms 22:1-2 AMP**

This challenges our faith, as we feel and find God to be far away, distant or insensitive to our demise. To be forsaken, ignored, or abandoned feels like God doesn't love us or care. To be forsaken, abandoned, ditched, discarded, is to be rejected. And people who feel rejected, end up rejecting other people; but if the feeling goes deeper it may result in feeling rejected by God – then the feeling of rejection becomes the excuse to blame God.

In fact, God is causing our faith to grow and go deeper with Him. Consequently, feelings have to be challenged, because they are a poor foundation for faith and this feeling of rejection, especially, because it goes to the root of being accepted. Without God's intervention of His silence our feelings can lead us to become *'double minded'* unstable in all we do. **James 1:7-8 YLT**

We all want to be accepted but our acceptance in God can only come by faith so that we please God. **Hebrews 11:6** This faith is conditional in that we must believe that He exists and that He rewards those who earnestly seek Him. Believing in the existence of God creates a foundation that is immovable, He is and always will be. *'Jesus is the same yesterday, today and forever.'* **Hebrews 13:8**

His unchanging nature means He is trustworthy and can be relied upon. Believing on this immovable rock causes us to be *'single minded'* and challenges the *'double mindedness,'* causing us to be unstable in all that we do. God's silence challenges our doubts that create instability and insecurity in our faith in Him. **James 1:6-8 YLT**

Can God be trusted? Can we put complete confidence in Him – having that conviction spoken of earlier, so that our Hope is sure and certain. If we are doubting we are saying that God cannot be trusted and therefore He cannot help us.

To trust God is to know God and that He can be depended upon. The journey of knowing God and deepening our relationship with Him takes time. It is not just in acquiring knowledge, but applying that knowledge to our daily lives. God has to take us through circumstances, so that we face up to our lack of knowledge and its application.

We work out our faith with fear and trembling – but God is the author of our faith. He began a good work and He will complete it until the day of Jesus Christ. **Philippians 1:6** We will be perfect just as your Father in Heaven is perfect. **Matthew 5:48**

But this perfection is positional, because of the sacrifice of Christ – but now, in this life, we have to contend with all its complications. Yet God enables us to overcome, *'In this world you will have tribulation, but be of good cheer I have over-*

come the world,' (**John 16:33**) and be victorious. **1 Corinthians 15:55-57 AMP**

'God saved us when we were sinners, yet loved us.' **Romans 5:8** He is still saving us and allowing us to serve Him, even though we still have a sinful nature and are prone to sinning. **Romans7:17-24** This is not a negative statement as some might think because our sinful nature is being refined and purified by an eternal God. **Daniel 12:10, 2 Corinthians 7:1**

A denial of this process of thinking that we are saved and free from our sin because of Christ's work on the cross, is to miss the process of sanctification. That is to miss the miracle saving power of God within and of seeing His ongoing transforming power at work in our lives. **Romans 12:1-2** This robs us of a living testimony to declare His works in and through us, as over-comers in Christ. **Matthew 24:13**

He is Creator (**Genesis1:1, Isaiah 40:28-31 AMP**) – a foundational truth about who God is – and as Creator; He is still creating that transforming power. So, the silence – or forsakenness – that we perceive, is God calling us to put our faith and trust in Him. We previously discussed that faith is the substance of what is not seen but it is also the substance of what we do not hear! Therefore, in the silence we are still called to stand in faith. Faith is the solid foundation we need to stand on.

God creates all life and His power working in us brings healing and our healing becomes the testimony of what Christ has done for us to share with others. **2 Corinthians 1:4**

So why did Christ say on the Cross, *'Why have you forsaken me?'* In our humanity, we only see from our perspective about our circumstances, but God sees from His perspective. Christ's humanity expressed His forsakenness, but Christ's deity was working out the purposes of God for our salvation. **Isaiah 52:13-53:12; 2 Corinthians 4:18** Silence from God's voice may feel as if we have been separated from God, but this is just a feeling, it is not reality! – because God has promised never to leave us or forsake us. **Hebrews 13:5 AMP**

Creating the world out of nothing means God can do anything – *'with God all things are possible.'* **Matthew 19:26** If God can do anything, He can overcome all our obstacles. This challenges our understanding and if our faith is limited to our understanding then it will fail us – God is not limited, we are! We may see no hope, no future, but God can and does miracles every day. This God that brought all things into existence, is the God who can be turned to in times of trouble. He is greater than any obstacle that we face. **1 John 4:4**

Dying on the cross as an innocent man, (**Isaiah 53**), this was a dark day – an understatement. We may suffer very dark days, some may face persecutions, threats to life, obstacles that seem insurmountable and we cannot see the way out. This is the time when we may feel the same as Christ, *'Why have you forsaken me?'* **2 Corinthians 4:7-12**

The Christ on the cross expressed His humanity as He felt the separation from His Father, as He took on the burden of paying the price for every sin committed here on earth. This separation revealed every thought and feeling that we may encounter when we experience a similar experience of trauma, and we do not receive the help that we desire, want and feel we need.

'Why have you forsaken me?' is based on a theological error and understanding of the purposes of God and His ways in dealing with His people. God's eternal perspective sees a bigger picture from beginning to end of our walk with Him.

Christ dying on the cross seemed an apparent disaster – the end of the good news of the gospel. It would appear that if Christ was the teacher of the new covenant this expectation and hope would end with Christ's death. No wonder the disciples were devastated and fled the scene. What would happen now? The cornerstone of the church has died – but this understanding is false, if viewed only from humanity's perspective. **Ephesians 2:20**

The end became the very beginning of the spread of the gospel to everyone. Christ's death released the Holy Spirit to come and reach many more people. This disaster was part of God's plan to reach the world with the gospel. So, was Christ forsaken? Yes, He died as part of God's greater purpose. But Christ's death set the people free to enable them to have access to God the Father. **Ephesians 2:11-22** Christ paid the price for sin, so that the anger of God was removed and a Holy God could relate to His people through the atoning blood of Christ. **Romans 3:25**

Christ's forsakenness opened the way to a deeper understanding of the greatness and purposes of God. Did Christ have to die? Yes, the son of God died for us, to set us free from our sinful nature. God understood the vulnerability of humanity and His plan was set in place before the foundation of the world, to save humanity. Christ's expression of forsakenness on the cross anticipated and identified with the forsakenness that we feel in those dark times, to prepare us that when we feel helpless and hopeless and can see no way out, Christ has gone before us.

We do not have a High Priest who is unable to sympathise with our weaknesses. **Hebrews 4:15 AMP** Christ knows what it is like to feel the above. He felt it and thought it too, as He expressed it in His humanity. But the Godhead is a hypostatic union – God is eternal and Christ, the son of God, means that Christ – who is equal with God – died for us. So, God the Father died for us. Except we know that God cannot die, so it was the humanity of Christ that died, not His deity.

Christ's humanity died and it was in this experience that he felt forsaken. God wants our humanity to die too, our corrupt mistrust of God to die. *'For me to live is Christ, to die is gain.'* **Philippians 1:21** We must die so that Christ can live in and through us. The God of the impossible is a God that can be trusted. Our thoughts and feelings need to be challenged by God's Holy Spirit – to trust God and not our flesh, completely, in everything that He sends us.

This is why it's so important to read God's word that brings us encouragement and comfort, of how He came through for all those who trust in Him. Forsaken, yes, but only for a season for God to do His work in us – to refine us and mature us, to be the disciples He needs us to be. This then becomes our testimony to reach the world. Forsaken, yes, but not forgotten, not abandoned, not discarded, or ditched. The truth of God is, He is faithful and believers are forever saved – none shall pluck them from His hand, NONE! **John 17:12 AMP** Nothing can separate us from His love. **Romans 8:28-29 AMP**

Even in times of trouble, God is at work. *'Where does my help come from?'* (**Psalm 121, Hebrews 13:5-6. AMP**) – from heaven? So, we look not to what we see or hear, to our circumstances, or what others may or may not say? We do not need to wait for a *'prophetic word',* when we already have His word. We do not rely on Asshur, Egypt, or horses? **Hosea 14; Psalms 20:7** We do not look to external help, because we put our trust in Almighty God. What is your *'Egypt'* you turn to? Any reliance on a substitute for God's help will fail us. God is the only one who can help us, our Hope is in Him.

Our faith is a gift from God, but needs to be exercised. In our sin we may feel weak and faithless but the faith God gives us is enough to take us through. **Timothy 2:11-13** The simile of the mustard seed, so small, but grows so big, is a reminder that however we may measure and estimate our *'faith level',* it is enough for us. The measure of faith is not judged by human standards, because it is given to us individually and in the measure that we need for that moment in time.

We need to encourage each other to have faith, but not in the way it is sometimes used, as a derogatory statement – that you are failing as a believer. *'Just believe and you will receive whatever it is you have asked for.'* This is a promise only given if we do not ask wrongly, for our own pleasures, or if the prayer is *'in God's will.'* **James 4:3; 1 John 5:14**

God's will is not always the same as we think. God's will led Jesus by the Holy Spirit to be tempted in the wilderness! **Matthew 4:1ff** God's will may lead us into dark times for the perfecting of our faith and character. This is not what we want to hear, and try to dismiss it, but God will have His will done anyway. Who are we to challenge God as to His purposes in our lives? **Job 42:2**

6 – Stress of walking in faith, being in faith, living by faith!

Walking in faith may increase stress internally, especially if we feel or are told that we are not living in faith, lack faith, or are not being faithful. This accusation and judgement from others, may become internalised within the accused. Being told that *'you may lack faith'* is a non-acceptance of other believers and comes across as a projection of superiority towards them.

It is a prideful attempt to belittle others which has the effect of discouraging others to exercise the faith they have. It creates a *'them and us scenario'* and can be seen in church settings. Sometimes only the *'spiritual,'* or *'seen to be faithful,'* are allowed to serve God in the church.

This segregation and ostracisation goes against the principle of *'the body of Christ'* in the church. All are needed in the service of Christ. To ostracise and remove members from the body is the same as saying *'we have no need of you'*; it is un-biblical and unscriptural. **1 Corinthians 14** This view of unity comes out of compliance to only one way of viewing the church and its vision.

Yet, some leaders seem to use their position to get rid of, or sideline, those individuals who do not seem to come up to their esteemed human standard. This is spiritual abuse that comes out of legalism and a gross misuse of power and authority in the church. To be dismissed and disrespected for *'not attaining the acceptable standard'* is insulting to God and judges the offending members as having little or no worth or any value. Misuse may be spiritualised as *'protecting the house'* – whatever that means – but misuse is often practised and is further evidence of spiritual abuse.

There may be times when this approach is necessary as in **Galations 6:1**, but this can be used, and disguised as, non-compliance to the leaders' point of view.

Only God gives leaders authority and power to fulfil their positions. **John 19:11 YLT** Power and authority belong to God; it is given and delegated by God and therefore each leader is accountable for the way they have exercised this privilege as they express it towards God's people. **Ezekiel 34:1-4 AMP** But every shepherd that is false will be exposed, and every shepherd that has used the sheep as prey will be held accountable. And God will rescue the sheep and will search out the abused, and He will gather them again under Godly leadership.

God will heal the hurting and strengthen the weak again. God will do the judging *'between sheep and sheep'!* And this type of spiritual abuse has been exposed before in many sad cases; where leaders have overstepped the mark and clearly lost their love and care for God's people.

'Let this mind be in you which was also in Christ Jesus, who, being in the form of God, did not consider it robbery to be equal with God, but made Himself of no reputation, taking the form of a bondservant, and coming in the likeness of men. And being found in appearance as a man, He humbled Himself and became obedient to the point of death even the death of the cross.' **Philippians 2:5ff**

He made Himself of NO REPUTATION. His purpose on earth was to represent God to the people, not to make a name for Himself.

Good leaders do not have to *'lord it over the sheep'*. Abusive authority removes the protection from the sheep *and* the leaders. Coercive submission creates an environment where that leader becomes dictatorial, dictating to the sheep as to what they can or cannot do. Jesus, the Good Shepherd, never imposed His authority on others. **Matthew 19:16-22** He knew who He was and was secure in Himself. Jesus was secure in His Heavenly Father so handled power and authority correctly.

Chapter 6 – Stress of walking in faith, being in faith, living by faith!

Bad leaders reveal themselves in the relationships they have with their members. Their relationship angst projects their insecurities and lack of self-awareness towards others. It suggests their lack of self-identity when they try to impose their authority onto the members. These leaders over-compensate in hiding behind their insecurities, by presenting themselves as overly authoritative because of their spirituality.

Good shepherds come alongside the sheep, provide for them encouraging them, restoring them and guiding them. In Israel we learn that the shepherds lead their sheep from the front (**Psalm 23 AMP**), they don't have to drive them or coerce them to submission.

Coercive control creates a situation of fear and of oppression amongst the sheep. The leader then errs towards cultic behaviour and ends up becoming a *'cult leader'*. Jesus Christ, the Good Shepherd, did not need to suppress the sheep; He came to build them up not destroy them. He came not to condemn them but to save them. **John 3:17**

It is astonishing and sad to realise and be made aware that we now have *'cult leaders'* in the church! Time reveals their true intentions that is manifest in their response to the believers in the church, hiding behind their *'spirituality'* and position.

Unity from this above view comes out of compliance to only one way of seeing the church and its vision. This type of unity is legalistic, restrictive and limits the vast resource and giftings that God has given to the body of Christ and therefore, is blatantly wrong. The Scripture speaks of *'distinctive varieties'* – speaking of many ways of service. If the sheep are funnelled into one vision of service, this is not freeing the members and suppresses God's creative work amongst believers. **1 Corinthians 12:4-7 AMP** It is a lack of respect and recognition for the different, diversities of ministries and giftings that the sheep have been given by God.

'Are we all apostles, teachers, evangelists, pastors,' etc? **1 Corinthians 12:29-30** NO, we are not, and to enforce a particular vision or ministry is *'cult-like'* and needs to be challenged. Individuals' ministries can support the vision; however, if the vision is ungodly, based in alternative motives, there may be a conflict between the vision expressed and individuals' ministries within the church context.

If the leader enforcing this abuse won't listen to wise counsel it will be a *'fool's errand'*. If this happens, then the sheep must protect themselves and find another place to be fed – a place where they are accepted and loved for who they are and can practise the ministries and giftings God has given to them.

Our loyalty is first and foremost to God, not people. **Exodus 20:1-2 YLT** Loyalty to bad shepherds diminishes the believer to be less than what God has created them to be. Good shepherds will encourage each believer to be all that God wants them to be.

It is possible an individual could be deceived about the ministry and gift they say they have or want. If this is true then there will be no positive fruit from it, therefore the leader who is secure in his position and within themselves does not need to be overly concerned. God can and will correct that individual's erroneous thinking.

Or, if there are several believers with the same ministry and giftings then they can all be accommodated for. There is no need for competition in the church, yet, we find this is not unusual; John's disciples and Jesus' disciples were in dispute against the methodology of purification and baptisms. **John 3:22-26**

To emphasise one believer's gift over another sets up rivalry and division within the church. A man can receive nothing unless it has been given to him from heaven. Therefore, believers need to be content with the gifts God has given to them. The purpose of the ministries and gifts is to promote God, not ourselves. *'He must increase I must decrease',* therefore we should see more of God within and less of ourselves. **John 3:30**

However, if a ministry or gift is denied, or suppressed, this will increase frustration within the body of Christ and the sheep will feel alienated and not welcomed in that part of the body. This is an avoidable scenario if the leader surrounds themself with wise leaders. However, it is in the nature of insecure leaders to surround themselves with *'yes people',* and only those that say what they want to hear.

Therefore, the attribution of wisdom is a subjective projection onto the *'yes people',* who have been given positions of leadership. If so, they may say what the Pastor wants to hear, – especially if their status or position in the church is vulnerable. **1 Kings 12:3ff**

'Itching ears' (**2 Timothy 3-4**) is not just a problem for the hearers, erring towards teaching they like, but also is a problem with insecure leaders too, leading them to be entrenched in their approach towards the sheep in the body of Christ. The positive reinforcement from the *'yes group'* encourages the Pastor to continue in their approach without being challenged. This means that the damage to the sheep will continue, until it becomes so bad it is exposed, usually by media outlets.

Many sheep have been damaged and hurt by this determined and fixed response and it must be addressed. Our agenda must be from God and if it is, then it doesn't need to be enforced, God will bring it to pass. **Job 42:2** If it is not, and is just a passionate appetite to see a church move in a particular direction, then it will open the door to spiritual abuses.

Insecure leaders will have to use manipulative tools to coerce the believers into a particular direction; this is a poor use of leadership skills and is negative manipulation. However, if the vision and agenda is of God then believers can be encouraged to move in a particular direction. Leaders can influence this direction carefully with positive reinforcement that doesn't need to be forced in a *'My way or the Highway'* approach!

Jesus Christ made Himself of NO REPUTATION and unfortunately a man-made, driven, revivalist agenda produces a condemning self-seeking leadership. To be revived has never been about quantity, it is always internal and about character and integrity that God builds within the individual believer. **Joel 2:12-18, Hosea 14:3ff**

Leaders that want to pursue quantity over quality are more concerned with their own reputation and achievements. If the church is not built on God's foundation, it may appear to be successful but *'all that glistens is not gold';* the dross will be burnt up in the end. **1 Corinthians 3:11-15 AMP**

Jesus Christ did not EXALT HIMSELF – He didn't need to. He humbled Himself and it was God who exalted Him. He came to serve the people. **Matthew 20:25-28, Mark 10:35-45** He sacrificed Himself and gave up His life for the people. We need faith to discern and recognise who are good or bad leaders.

Synopsis of a cult leader: (***Combating cult mind control*, Hassan. S. 2016**).

- Leader's perceived view of doctrine is to be accepted and this is the one and only truth.
- It sets up a process of the participant creating a new identity that distrusts their own authentic self.
- Sets up a them v. us scenario, as no criticism of the leader or their ideals is to be disputed.
- Group members adopt an elitist mentality, feeling special, chosen by God to lead others into their truth.
- Members are kept busy, made to feel responsible for the group members, that focuses on performance orientation and group think.

- Individuality is suppressed over group think and conformity to group is good.

- Reality is distorted in preference to *'what the leader states'* creating a dependency scenario.

- Group members held in compliance by using accusative emotions – guilt, shame and fear – to expose wrong thinking and behaviours (sometimes called *'shepherding'*, or *'discipling,'* in some church groups).

- Members are temporarily *'love bombed'* to cement them into the group. All old relationships or old ways of thinking for the self are cut off and/or ridiculed and mocked, to shame the individual.

- Behaviours are controlled by rewards and punishments. Competition is encouraged to increase performance productivity.

- Previous contacts are distorted from their past, present and projected onto the future. The present being bombarded with increasing pressure and demands for the group to be promoted. The future is when they will be rewarded for promotion when they have reached the heights of performance and loyalty to the cult leader.

- The group family is the only family to adhere to and fear is installed that if the member leaves they will be punished.

CONFORMITY therefore in the body of Christ is not helpful to the life of the church and gives leaders a disproportionate amount of power. Many leaders are unable to use power correctly and so their authority within the church becomes abusive. *'Power tends to corrupt and absolute power corrupts absolutely,'* (**Lord Acton**)

The stress that is evoked encourages a performance orientated, works righteousness, walk with God, to adhere to the demands of the leader's vision. The performance is the perception and pressure exerted on the body of Christ, to make themselves more *'spiritual'* by doing the right things: singing the right worship songs, praying in the right way, or reading the right translation of the Bible, or believers who are open to the Spirit of God can *'speak in tongues,'* etc. Or engaging in works righteousness by being *'encouraged'* to serve in the church, possibly with the assumption of a leadership role. **Luke 10:38-42**

Jesus said, *'one thing is needed and Mary has chosen that good part, which will not be taken away from her'!* Works righteousness can open the door to pride; with the intention of showing others *'how good they are by their service in the church,'* but pride always goes before a fall, we are told. **Proverbs 16:18**

The damage done, if the believer is forced to leave the church, can interfere with the believer's relationship with God and of church itself. This can lead to people being put off of church and they may become isolated which will challenge their faith in God as well.

So, the frustrations, disappointments, disillusionments, anxieties, contributes to the stresses experienced in church life. These must be addressed in a therapeutic way, to enable the believer to grow in maturity, grace and faith. When the damage experienced is addressed therapeutically, this can be a learning curve, to engage and understand God's purposes and handle church life more successfully.

Where you have people you have problems. So, it is not surprising that the Body of Christ, which has many individuals will raise issues within church and outside of church life. But what we learn from dealing with the effect of those problems is what strengthens us and motivates us to continue in the faith and with church.

7 – Faith for church

Despite the stresses that involvement with church life can produce; the community of the church is an amazing global organism that reaches to everyone – whatever, age, gender, intellect, maturity etc. It sustains individuals from birth to death. (**J. John**) It incorporates a range of lifestyles to show the love of Christ.

The gates of hell will not prevail against her! It is God's church and will succeed in whatever way God decides. Christ states that, '*on this rock I will build MY Church.*' **Matthew 16:18** The rock is the revelation that Christ is the Son of God and He will build His Church and the gates of Hell will not overcome Him. But it references Peter as his name means *'rock'* too, but Christ is the Rock, the *'stone'* that the builder's rejected. **1 Peter 2:4**

To be fixated in how the church is to be shaped is to adopt an extremist, rigid attitude. It doesn't take into account that God's idea of church is being manifested in various ways. There are traditional, huge monoliths, to smaller buildings, many particular denominations, to groups that meet in houses.

The varieties and expressions of church life enable every individual believer to find a church that is suited to their preferences. To manipulate church in a particular way, is to limit the expression of God to different believers. Within these different types there are numerous types of personalities, liturgies, times and places where church congregates.

Revival of believers will not happen in one particular type of church. God loves His church and can revive any church at any time He chooses and He uses whom He chooses anywhere. To try and manipulate a scenario, with the right leaders, right atmosphere, right worship expression, or type of people to bring in a revival, is a man-made approach.

You may have heard of *'messy church'* – an innovation to encourage younger people into the church; but messy church is a real thing, for everyone who attends church. Not all those personalities fit together, except, by a miracle – for example you may have extrovert personalities rubbing alongside reticent, indecisive personalities. But there is no one personality type that is acceptable. God has called all types of personalities to receive salvation and these different types may be in the same church or group. This obviously may create difficulties with relationships in the church.

Conformity addresses this issue by wanting all believers in church to be the same, believe the same, express their faith and service towards the same end – but this approach is an affront to the scriptural teaching of the body of Christ, already discussed above.

Real unity must come out of a recognition and acceptance that all believers are given gifts and ministries that can contribute to the maturity of the body of Christ. **Ephesians 1:22-23; 2:19-22, 4:16, 1 Corinthians 12 AMP**

God's plan sets up the fullness and expression of His love within His church; enabling everyone with the opportunity to grow and be nurtured into a deeper walk with Christ. His plan develops individual believers to come into a deeper knowledge and understanding about God and His church. This equips them to be the witnesses needed to fulfil the Great Commission. **Matthew 28:19-20**

Some plant, some water, but God gives the increase – or do we follow men? **1 Corinthians 1 :12, 3:5-9** Consequently, the platform for building the body of Christ must always be on HIM and not on any other type of *'wisdom'* in how a church must grow. If it is a revivalist agenda that inhibits a believer's contributions to the body, it will always be wrong. The *'one man ministry'* was rejected some time ago.

God has called *'a multitude'* – *'all nations, tribes, peoples and tongues, standing before the throne and before the Lamb ...'* **Revelation 7:9-10 AMP** *'And it shall come to pass afterward that I will pour out MY Spirit on all flesh, your sons and your daughters, your old men shall dream dreams, your young men shall see visions, also on MY menservants and my maid-servants, I will pour out My spirit in those days ...'* **Joel 2:28** In other words, God is inclusive, not exclusive, in His criteria that all believers will be touched by God, to serve the church, both within and without in the community.

However, at the same time, there must be a cohesive framework for believers to be different within the same construct. Many parts but one body, to the profit of all. And one Lord, one faith, one baptism, one God and Father of all, who is above all and through all and in you all. **Ephesians 4:5-6**

So, if any part is ignored, suppressed, disregarded, then the body of Christ suffers and stays immature and unstable. Subsequently, we must have UNITY, BUT IN DIVERSITY, ONENESS BUT DIFFERENT PARTS, TOGETHER BUT SEPARATE, THE SAME BUT UNIQUE. (**Rivera**)

To obtain this completeness of same, but different, is a work of God, who will work through good leaders to bring this together – a miracle indeed! But what is impossible with man is possible with God. **Matthew 19:26**

So, we are a long way off from the goal above which means that many people may get hurt by the church from relational conflicts and from authoritative church leaders. But, as we all know, our sinful nature is still being refined, being changed from glory to glory. **2 Corinthians 3:18 AMP**

8 – Theotherapeutic healing

The church is God's design to enable us to draw us to Himself by the challenges we navigate within it. It also reveals who we are as individuals. We come up against others who may irritate, annoy, frustrate, disappoint, cause disillusionment. etc. **Proverbs 27:17** This is a good thing as it exposes how God needs us to grow up in Him and mature within ourselves. However, God also uses external circumstances to draw us closer to Himself as well.

There is no one time fix-all therapy, or formula, but we have biblical principles that we can apply. Each believer faces relationships in different ways – we are unique in how we process our circumstances, our thought processes and emotional responses to them. But it is a given that all conflict is relational.

We do not relate to objects in the same way as we relate to human beings. To do this we must think clearly and rationally so that we can address these challenges. Therefore, we need to explore who taught us how to react and respond in the way that we do.

Thinking is hard work, that's why few people do it, so we try to opt for the easy option and avoid it by using defence mechanisms and cognitive distortions. **(Einstein A., Scott Peck M.)** These mind mechanisms may be conscious or not but inhibit the healing process. And it must be a process, so that God can heal the mind mechanisms that we use – for example, avoidance, or sublimation, as defence mechanisms that seek to escape the pain in dealing with difficult relationships. We must recognise and address our emotional responses to the challenges and discover the origin and root of bitterness within. **Hebrews 12:15**

Therefore, we need to address the emotional angst that exposed the mind mechanisms associated with it, so we can be healed in body, soul and spirit. **1 Thessalonians 5:23 AMP** So, this is done by first identifying the relationships that have caused the emotional response – e.g. an overbearing father – then choosing to forgive them specifically for the conflict that the individual experienced.

Forgiveness means I'm letting go of the harm that was caused and choosing not to demand they pay a price to make up for what they did or did not do. Then choose to accept them as they are and not to change that individual or the circumstance where it originated. Then surrender that individual up to God. Surrendering to God means I'm going to give the offender to God, so that He can work in their lives as He chooses. **Romans 12:19**

However, while God is free to do His work, we must use *Theotherapeutic Indifference* and after dealing with the distress to leave the conflict in the past, and make a decision to move forward with our lives. This means not to get stuck, or in a rut, but to learn from it and move on, learning and growing in God.

Therefore, first leave your gift at the altar, make amends within, as to why there was a conflict and deal with the root of it. **Matthew 5:24** There is no altar today, so we make things right with God first, so that God can heal us internally and transform our lives. **Romans 12:1-2** Then the relationship can be healed externally, if that is possible. But first the individual must make things right before God, before any attempt can be made to heal a relationship externally.

After dealing with the relationship conflict the individual must substitute the relationship with love. Love is the glue that holds everything together. When we make a choice to love the individual involved it changes our perspective on them, healing the relationship.

This therapeutic approach is not prescriptive and can be a challenge. Therefore, it is helpful for the individual to share these relational conflicts with a trained Theotherapist, because *'the heart is deceptively wicked above all else'*. **Jeremiah 17:4** We sometimes hit *'blind spots'* and need counsellors who are outside of our circumstances to see the wood from the trees. A trained Theotherapist can bring clarity to this confusion experienced in getting to the root of the angst. (To find Theotherapists see ***Bibliography***).

This Theotherapeutic process takes courage and humility on the part of the individual. But it is needed within the church setting today, so that we do not hide behind our spiritual face, suppressing internal distress. It is God's desire to heal us all, in order for us to know and love Him better and to love others. **1 Peter 1:22**

Conclusion

Psalm 139 – we have all been created unique in God's eyes. God is gracious loving and is abundant in mercy and long-suffering. He is bringing together the masterpiece of His Bride by making her ready for Christ's return. His plan has already been accomplished, but the Bride on earth is not perfected yet. Therefore, God is changing His Bride – the church – by causing her to return to a state of being perfected in love for when He sends Jesus to return for her. Until then the body of Christ is being humbled, in which every part is being drawn together to become a living temple.

The church becoming the epitome of inclusivity – every tribe, every nation, every tongue, every people, every race, every colour, every personality type, every age, both male and female; incorporated into the Body of Christ. Salvation for all who believe in Jesus Christ as their Lord and Saviour.

Transforming the minds and hearts to be like Christ through a process of accepting and surrendering to God's plan and purpose for each individual. Regaining the meaning of our first love for God through a therapeutic process helps us to rely on God to supply all our needs. This dependence leads us to grow and mature in a deeper understanding and relationship with Him.

As we experience God's Agape love – a true love – we can begin to experience a little of what it might have been like to live in the Garden of Eden with God. An idea of perfection in acceptance in the context of Agape love and enjoying more peaceful relationships with each other, as we build each other up in the community of the church. And reaping the benefits of the life that God intended for us before sin entered the world. So, we look forward to the day when we can eternally live with our Saviour.

Come Lord Jesus, come. Maranatha.

About the author:

Dr Heather Owen is a retired nurse, RGN, and has a BSc (Hons) in *Psychology* and an MSc in *Abnormal and Clinical Psychology* from Swansea University. She has been married for forty-one years to Rev. Chris Owen and has three grown up sons.

In 1990 she started training in Theotherapy and recently completed a *Doctorate in Theotherapy* (TT.D) – awarded by *Christian Counselling International*, based in Puerto Rico. The principles of Theotherapy have enabled the pursuit of the above educational achievements and brought healing, to build solid relationships with others.

She is an experienced Theotherapist and trainer and currently teaches and counsels in the modality of Theotherapy – online and in person. This has allowed many people to find the healing that they need, and to go on and pursue their own callings in ministry.

The pursuit of the Theotherapy modality has also been helpful in her own spiritual development and maturity, which is still an ongoing adventure. She says, *'It is a joy to see how Theotherapy works in and heals individuals lives.'*

Heather loves Wimbledon, playing the piano, singing and trying to keep fit! She also has a love of reading the Word, studying and learning from others more learned than herself, both in the theological and secular world.

The first book in the *Joy Series*, ***The Bride's Blemish***, was published by **Precious Oil Publications** in 2024.

This book is the second in the *Joy Series*.

Acknowledgements

To all my family members, husband and friends, who have taken time and effort out from their busy lives to encourage and support this endeavour. Without them I probably wouldn't have started at all.

Love you all.

Oh, and thanks to Covid restrictions for all that free time to start my first book in the ***Joy Series***.

And acknowledgements to *Precious Oil Publications* for their patience.

Bibliography

All scripture references are from the **New King James Version**, unless otherwise stated.

Amplified Bible (1965). Zondervan Publishing House, grand rapids, Michigan, USA.

Arthur J. New King James Version, Study Bible. (1997). Word Bibles, Thomas Nelson co., Nashville

Berry R. (2000). ***Jung. A beginner's Guide***. Hodder & Stoughton. ISBN 0-340-78055 X

Christian Counselling International: *https://christiancounsellinginternational.org*

English standard Version. (2001). Crossway Publishers.

Einstein A. https://quotefancy.com/quote/763409/Albert-Einstein-Thinking-is-hard-work-that-s-why-so-few-do-it. Accessed 12/11/25.

Fromm E. (1956). ***The Art of Loving, an enquiry into the nature of love***. Harper & Brothers.

Hassan S. (2016). Combating cult mind control. Freedom of Mind Press, Newton, MA

John J. (2022). Canon of Coventry. http://celebrationofhope.sg/ Accessed 12/11/25.

Nelson T. New King James Version (2018). Thomas Nelson Publisher. ISBN-13 978-0718075583

Scott Peck M. (1999). ***The road less travelled and beyond***. Ryder Publisher. ISBN-13: 978-0712670760

Rivera, Rev. M., (M.Div., MD, TT.D), Christian Counselling International, San Juan, Puerto Rico.

Strongs concordance. (Strong J. 1968).

The American Heritage Dictionary of the English Language. 5th Edition. (2012). Houghton Mifflin Company. Randon House Inc.

Young R. Youngs Literal Translation. (2012) Benediction classics, Oxford. ISBN: 978-1-781-232-4

The Bride's Blemish

(Book #1 of the ***Joy Series***)

Dr. Heather Owen

This short book is for Christian believers who wish to pursue deeper, loving relationships that are truly satisfying and fulfilling.

Strong platonic relationships with the opposite sex will encourage the foundation for future strong marital relationships, which will allow individuals to reflect God's design for marriage.

Other books from ***Precious Oil Publications:***

Fiction & non-fiction by ***Raymond McCullough:***

Six Hours fiction series,
(based on bible prophecy):

The *Arrows* bible prophecy series
(hitting one prophetic target at a time):

Bible prophecy identifying end-time Babylon

Testimonies from around Ireland

Scripts from *Celtic Roots Radio* show

Fiction by ***Gerry McCullough:***

available from ***Amazon*** worldwide

www.ingramcontent.com/pod-product-compliance
Lightning Source LLC
LaVergne TN
LVHW022025200926
848481LV00007B/2545
9781738436552